AFRICAN AMERICAN LEADERS OF COURAGE

JACKIE ROBINSON

KRISTEN SUSIENKA

New York

Published in 2020 by The Rosen Publishing Group, Inc.
29 East 21st Street, New York, NY 10010

Copyright © 2020 by The Rosen Publishing Group, Inc.

All rights reserved. No part of this book may be reproduced in any form without permission in writing from the publisher, except by a reviewer.

First Edition

Editor: Kristen Susienka
Book Design: Michael Flynn

Photo Credits: Cover, pp. 1, 5, 19 Photo File/Hulton Archive/Getty Images; series background Kharchenko Rusian/Shutterstock.com; p. 7 Everett Historical/Shutterstock.com; pp. 9, 11 (inset) Archive Photos/Getty Images; p. 11 (main) Bettmann/Getty Images; p. 13 Sports Studio Photos/Getty Images; p. 15 Sporting News/Getty Images; p. 17 Transcendental Graphics/Getty Images; p. 21 (main) JonathanCollins/Shutterstock.com; p. 21 (inset) Icon Sportswire/Getty Images.

Library of Congress Cataloging-in-Publication Data

Names: Susienka, Kristen, author.
Title: Jackie Robinson / Kristen Susienka.
Description: New York : PowerKids Press, [2020] | Series: African American
   leaders of courage | Includes index.
Identifiers: LCCN 2019011237| ISBN 9781725308428 (pbk.) | ISBN 9781725308442
   (library bound) | ISBN 9781725308435 (6 pack)
Subjects: LCSH: Robinson, Jackie, 1919-1972–Juvenile literature. | African
   American baseball players–Biography–Juvenile literature. | Baseball
   players–United States–Biography–Juvenile literature.
Classification: LCC GV865.R6 S96 2020 | DDC 796.357092 [B] –dc23
LC record available at https://lccn.loc.gov/2019011237

Manufactured in the United States of America

CPSIA Compliance Information: Batch #CWPK20. For Further Information contact Rosen Publishing, New York, New York at 1-800-237-9932.

CONTENTS

Breaking Barriers. 4
A Different World 6
Jackie Grows Up. 8
A College Athlete 10
In the Army 12
Baseball Business 14
Joining the Dodgers 16
In the Big Leagues 18
Jackie Keeps Going. 20
The Life of Jackie Robinson 22
Glossary 23
Index 24
Websites 24

Breaking Barriers

Baseball is an important sport in America. Many people like playing it and watching games. Baseball brings people together. Jackie Robinson was a very important baseball player. He broke down **barriers** and changed the game forever.

A Different World

In the 1940s and 1950s, the United States had lots of rules that kept people apart. White people and black people couldn't go to the movies together. They couldn't play sports together. They couldn't eat together. **Segregation** affected many people's lives.

Jackie Grows Up

Jackie Robinson was born in 1919 in Cairo, Georgia. When he was one, his family moved to Pasadena, California. His dad left when he was young. His mom worked hard to raise the family. Jackie and his brother Mack were talented **athletes** in school.

A College Athlete

Jackie went to UCLA for college. He played many sports and was a star athlete. In college, he met a woman named Rachel. She would later marry Jackie. In 1941, however, the United States entered World War II. Jackie joined the army.

Rachel and Jackie Robinson

In the Army

By 1943, Jackie had become an officer in the army. One day, though, he was sitting on a military bus. The driver told him to move to the back because he was black. Jackie refused. He went to court and the court threw out the charges.

Baseball Business

Jackie left the army in 1944 with an **honorable discharge**. He started to play sports again. In 1945, he joined an African American baseball team called the Kansas City Monarchs. People started to notice him. One of these people was Branch Rickey.

Joining the Dodgers

Branch Rickey was the Brooklyn Dodgers' president and manager, or leader. The Dodgers were a **major league** team. Branch wanted to **integrate** the Dodgers. He signed Jackie to play baseball. On April 15, 1947, Jackie played his first game for the Dodgers.

In the Big Leagues

Jackie was the first African American to play major league baseball. It wasn't easy. People bullied him. Rachel and his teammates helped him stay calm. With the Dodgers, Jackie became a hero. He played with the team for 10 seasons.

Jackie Keeps Going

After he left baseball, Jackie took part in the U.S. **civil rights movement**. In 1962, he became the first black person in the Baseball Hall of Fame. Jackie Robinson died in 1972. He was a hero who taught many people to break down barriers.

Baseball Hall of Fame

THE LIFE OF JACKIE ROBINSON

1919 — Jackie Robinson is born.

1942 — Jackie joins the U.S. Army.

1945 — Jackie starts playing for the Kansas City Monarchs.

1947 — Jackie Robinson joins the Brooklyn Dodgers.

1972 — Jackie Robinson dies.

GLOSSARY

athlete: Someone who's very good at playing sports.

barrier: Something that blocks someone from doing something.

civil rights movement: A time in the United States during the 1950s and 1960s when people fought for equal rights for all Americans.

honorable discharge: A formal release from the military after faithful service.

integrate: To make a person or group part of a larger group.

major league: The top level of a professional sport, especially baseball.

segregation: The separation of people based on race, class, or ethnicity.

INDEX

A
army, 10, 12, 14, 22

B
Baseball Hall of Fame, 20, 21
Brooklyn Dodgers, 16, 18, 22

C
Cairo, 8

K
Kansas City Monarchs, 14, 22

P
Pasadena, 8

R
Rickey, Branch, 14, 16
Robinson, Mack, 8
Robinson, Rachel, 10, 11, 18

U
UCLA, 10

W
World War II, 10

WEBSITES

Due to the changing nature of Internet links, PowerKids Press has developed an online list of websites related to the subject of this book. This site is updated regularly. Please use this link to access the list: www.powerkidslinks.com/AALC/robinson